Ta

Coping With Grief Of A Loved One

After A Suicide

Grieving The Devastation And Loss Of Someone Who Took Their Own Life.

How Long Does The Heartache Last?

Anthea Peries

Disclaimer This book is not intended to substitute physicians or legal professionals' professional legal or medical advice. Please always seek professional advice concerning your own circumstances.

Introduction

I am so sorry for your loss. It must be so devastating to lose a loved one to suicide. With so many questions left unanswered, how do you move forward from the heartbreak of the whole situation. You feel completely traumatised and paralysed.

This book will give an insight into what to do when someone commits suicide. How do you grieve. Understanding your feelings and accepting what has happened; answering questions along the way and how you are not alone and that support is available to you, especially with help from God.

What To Do When Someone Commits Suicide?

The reality of losing someone to suicide can be tricky. What helps one person cope is likely to help another, but what will make your grief more manageable? These are the answers you'll find right here in this book, which covers everything from understanding your feelings and accepting the loss—to finding support and making a positive change.

You feel alone, but you're falling apart.

"I just don't feel like I'm getting better," says Jane, 39. "I've been through five months of grief therapy, and I've learned all about the five stages of grief and the importance of keeping an open mind—but nothing seems to help. I'm not crying all the time as I did initially, but I still cry almost every time my kids leave for school in the morning. And when we had our annual family picnic last month, and everyone was laughing together and having a good time, I just sat there—like a zombie—because just looking at them made me want to cry. What's wrong with me? I just don't understand. I want to get better, but I'm not sure how to do it."

If you've lost a child, parent, or loved one to suicide and feel hopeless and depressed or just not yourself and don't know why you're not alone.

The death of a loved one by suicide is devastating for all family members, especially parents, children and siblings who are left behind. You're not overreacting or under-reacting to your feelings; they're normal reactions for someone who has experienced such an unthinkable event in their life. And, just as it's normal for you to feel sad and depressed, it's also typical for friends and family who have tried to offer their support and love to feel helpless and frustrated at the pain they see you going through.

Although several months or even years may have passed since your loved one died, the shock you're experiencing is a temporary reaction to a sudden and shocking loss. As time goes on—and the shock subsides—you will be able to better deal with your grief.

But until then, keep in mind that there are steps you can take to make coping with your grief easier. "*Don't wait too long before getting help*," said one doctor with a PhD, a licensed marriage and family therapist from Boca Raton, Fla., who specializes in grief and loss issues.

"*Getting help early on will help you cope, find answers to your questions, make decisions about your future and be better able to enjoy life again.*"

If the thought of talking about your loved one with another person feels awkward or overwhelming, it's OK to say that you need someone to talk to but not right now or that you'd rather talk about it yourself than share your feelings with anyone else. Just talking through these feelings is an essential step in beginning the healing process. And remember to call on your support system for help—in whatever form you need it. This individual may be a friend, family member, clergy person or counsellor.

If you don't feel comfortable talking about your loved one with others—or if you're not sure if what you're going through is normal; remember, there are other ways to cope.

You can do many things to honour and remember your loved one, according to One doctor. "*It's also important to reconnect with life by honouring the dreams and aspirations of the person who died. Get involved in activities that you enjoyed doing with your loved one. A simple way to begin is by making a list of the things you did together and then creating a new list of things you want to do together."*

You want to be angry, but it's not helping.

"I can't believe my brother died by suicide," says Melinda, 26. Melinda noted that people who have been through similar tragedies say they lose their best friends and, she lost her only brother, the one person she could talk to and trust with anything.

Melinda said she knew she was supposed to be grieving right now, but instead, she felt furious at him and the world. She said he was so young; he didn't deserve to die by suicide when there were so many things he wasn't even living for yet. She couldn't imagine how he could have done this to her. Her whole life felt so shattered. She was angry all the time; and feel like no one understood what it's like, and nothing would make it feel better for her. On top of everything else, their father died a year before, and when her brother died, all these feelings about her Dad came rushing back in ways they never did before. Melinda felt like she couldn't get a grip on her own life, and she didn't know who to turn to.

When people experience losing a loved one to suicide, they're likely to have a range of emotions, and they may even find themselves feeling angry. *"Anger is one of the most common reactions people have after someone close to them dies by suicide,"* says one doctor. *"And that's OK because that anger is a natural reaction."*

But, sometimes, family members become so preoccupied with their anger that they end up beating themselves up for feeling it. Yes, you've lost a loved one most tragically—but you shouldn't feel guilty about being angry about it.

According to one grief specialist doctor, it's widespread to feel anger, and it's a constructive emotion to help you heal. If you're not feeling angry, you're probably not paying enough attention. That said, if anger is interfering with your everyday life, that is, preventing you from functioning socially or at work—you should get help. Seek out a therapist or grief counsellor who is trained in dealing with suicide bereavement issues. Or just talk to a close friend or family member about what's going on. Being able to express your anger is often very good for your emotional well-being."

How do you understand your feelings about suicide and accepting the loss? This article will briefly discuss the author's challenge of coping with loss and accepting the suicide of a loved one. The book also includes some helpful suggestions from loved ones on how they managed in these times.

You are going to miss them, but you are not going to throw yourself into despair. The day may come when you can have the closure you need for your pain, but until then, take care of yourself so that you can still be there for them when they are ready. You never know what they might need from you.

It is challenging if the suicide of your loved one was sudden and unexpected, but it is still just as vital that you grieve. If someone commits suicide, there are always unanswered questions and regrets left behind. For some people, it will be easier to cope with their grief than for others. Each person must find the strength within themselves to do what they can to move on and continue their life after a loved one commits suicide.

Understanding Your Feelings And Accepting The Loss

Emotions, Feelings Explained

Coping with our emotions over the suicide during this time will be challenging. Feelings are an integral part of who we are as human beings, and they show us when we need to take action. They allow us to feel compassion for others and ourselves. We feel happy when something good happens to someone we care about and angry when someone harms someone or something that we love. It is essential for us to handle all of our feelings while caring for our loved ones. Sometimes people find their sadness overwhelming, but remember, it is OK to be sad. There is no timetable for grieving the loss of a loved one; each person must heal in their way at their own pace.

There are different kinds of feelings. When you are sad or angry, it often means that something impacts you on a deep level. Sometimes people are afraid to experience intense feelings because they feel vulnerable in the process. Sadness makes us feel helpless, and anger makes us feel uncomfortable because it can be frightening or overwhelming. You may want to hold onto your anger or sadness for a while to give yourself time to work through your feelings about this loss. It would help if you allowed yourself time to cope with your feelings about this loss so that you can get through them and move on with your life without becoming overwhelmed by sadness or anger.

Accepting Is Not Giving Up

There will always be a part of you who is sad about losing a loved one, but you need to accept it and move on. Sometimes we cling to our sadness or anger for too long, and when we finally let go, we find that it does not matter at all. When you finally understand your feelings about a loss, accepting them can be the most significant relief. Many people say that they will never be the same because they no longer feel like themselves; however, after time has passed, most people realize that they are better off without their loved ones. The healing process can take up to six months or more, so take care of yourself during this time.

When you work through your feelings and go through the healing process, you will find that with time, you can accept that all things must change and sometimes they need to change for the better. You may be sad about the loss of a person who meant so much to you, but there is more good out there than bad. We must keep reminding ourselves of this as we go through our grief, so we do not become overwhelmed by sadness or anger.

What Can I Do?

Do not allow unproductive thoughts to linger in your mind. It is helpful to set aside a specific time each day to think about things that make you feel better. Do some things that make you feel strong, and take control of your healing process.

To sum up, there is no need to jump into a new relationship after your loved one to replace them or heal your sadness. The healing process takes time, but eventually, you will find that losing someone to suicide is just as sad and painful as any other loss.

Comments From Loved Ones

I said in the last section, acceptance is vital and not giving in is key to moving forward. Here are some messages from people who have lost someone to suicide and were kind enough to share their experiences with us. Many people said that they found it helpful to talk about their loved one's death and how they felt about it with others who could relate.

I had a friend who I was told died of natural causes. When I found out the truth, it was tough to accept that he did not want to live. He didn't even leave a note or final words for us to remember him by. It has been ten years now, and I still think about him and wonder what he's doing now.

by Debs

I think it is hard because you don't get the chance to say goodbye or forgive them for their actions. Even when someone is terminally ill, there is still the chance to say goodbye.

by Adam

I grew up in a home where my Dad committed suicide. I thought I knew what it was like, but I didn't until it happened to me. Everyone's experience can be different, and it is hard not knowing how someone would want their loved one to be remembered or what they might leave behind. What helped me was talking to other people who had lost a parent as well. It helped me feel less alone and gave me something more to think about than the pain that overwhelms you in the moment of loss. It helped me separate my feelings about my Dad from the pain of losing him, and it gave me something to focus on besides myself. If that is not possible, just remember that this was a person's last choice and another reasonable person in their life. I know this is hard to believe sometimes, but it really can be helpful.

by Natalie

It was tough for me to hear that my best friend had decided to end his life. He was a kind man who had done many things for people, including buying groceries for a stranger when he didn't have the money himself. He was a good man, and I miss him a lot.

by Mina

I never knew how to deal with the situation because I had not lost someone close to me. I didn't realize that it is OK to mourn their death in the way you want. It is hard and painful not knowing if you will ever recover from such loss. It is much easier to put my feelings about death behind me and move on. Even though they hurt so much, I can live without them here on earth, just as we all must.

by Harry

I can only imagine how hard it must be to have your parents or family die. It is a very upsetting situation, but when someone that you love passes away, it is not the end of the world. It doesn't mean you aren't strong enough to deal with such loss in your life, just that you are not giving up on life. All do, but it is harder for people who have loved ones who died by suicide.

Helping Someone Cope With Suicidal Death

One of the most important things you and your loved ones can do is help the bereaved to cope with the loss of a loved one by suicide and, not just because they are in pain but also because it's a tragedy that needs to be addressed.

Of course, there are no simple answers because each situation is different. There are times when it's better if you don't say anything (especially if you feel unsure about what to say). But there are also times when you need to say something, such as when you know the person is thinking of doing self-harm, if the person is physically sick, or if they have made a desperate phone call.

(It's even possible that they will turn to you for support – this is primarily a possibility if they didn't feel they could talk to anyone else.) But at other times, there isn't much you can do except be there with them and listen.

That's why giving support in this way is so important. Sometimes it prevents people from making a suicide attempt, and sometimes it gives them the strength to carry on living. With your help and understanding, your loved ones can cope with their pain and their grief.

Remember, life does go on after losing a loved one to suicide. Life goes on for you and others around you. Some things will always make life worth living, however much you grieve. And some things will not help you survive – so don't push yourself to do them.

How do I cope with my grief?

Of course, no two people will cope in the same way after the death of a loved one from suicide. Some people feel like they have lost a part of themselves; others learn to lead better lives without the person who has died by suicide in their lives. The important thing is that most people can cope with dealing with death and grief. How well they manage and how quickly they recover is, as we all know, different for everyone.

People often feel guilty about what they should or shouldn't have done after the death of a loved one by suicide. But it's essential to get over these feelings so you can move on with your life. You may want to ask yourself if you have been able to let go of the guilt or work through your feelings about what happened before putting your life back together again.

How do people react to the suicide of a loved one?

When someone has a sudden, unexpected death from suicide, it can have a devastating effect on those left behind. People may feel angry and rejected by their loss. And sometimes, they even deny that their loved one committed suicide. They may feel guilty or embarrassed about it, and they may even take the blame for what happened.

But most people feel shocked and numb after a dramatic death such as suicide. It's important to remember that this is a natural reaction – it doesn't mean you don't care. And you mustn't avoid people if they ask you how you are.

Should I talk about the suicide of a loved one?

There is often a sense among friends and family that people should keep on living for the sake of the surviving family members. But there is also a strong argument for talking about the death of a loved one from suicide. It's essential to give practical help and support when needed, but it can also be very healing for those who have been left behind because they realize that other people have gone through the same thing – and they can feel less isolated.

The survivor of suicide has this choice – to deal with the pain by talking about it or keep it bottled up. If they don't talk about their loss, they may feel very alone in their grief, and they may feel less able to come to terms with what has happened. But if they can talk about it, this might help them heal faster from the tragedy. However, this requires support from their loved ones and others who care, which can be very hard for those left behind when someone dies by suicide.

It's also important to remember that not everyone feels able or willing to talk openly about suicidal deaths, especially if a person was particularly close or guilty. For most people, the end of a loved one by suicide can be a harrowing and profoundly distressing experience. But if the time is right, they should be allowed to talk about how they feel.

What can I do to help someone who's having suicidal thoughts?

When someone is having suicidal thoughts or making a suicide attempt, you usually want to stop them and make sure they are not taking any actions that may increase their risk of death. To do this, you need to know what these actions are and what might happen if you stop them. And it's essential not only for your safety but also for their safety – because you may affect their thinking patterns or ability to cope with everyday life. Therefore, it's a good idea to seek help from trained counsellors or other professionals who specialize in dealing with suicidal people.

But it is also crucial for you to know how best to support someone with suicidal thoughts.

Here are some things you can do:

• **listen and not judge** – make sure you're listening without judging (even though most of us are prone to doing that). Let them tell you what they are thinking and feeling. You don't have to agree but listen without whether or not what they say is true or how 'bad' they believe.

• **acknowledge their feelings** - let them know you are listening to them: "I hear you're feeling..."; "I'm so sorry it's taken me so long to reply. I've been swamped lately...."

• **offer support** – don't just listen, but make sure they know you are there for them: "You're quite right. It's worth fighting for your life." Or "You need someone like me when things get tough."

• **encourage help** – reassure them that support is available and tell them what to do if they are in immediate danger of dying (at a hospital, for example).

• **check their safety** – if they have access to drugs or alcohol, it's essential to check that they are not using them.

• **help them contact their GP** or other medical services. (Ask the person making the call to give you some information about whether this is an emergency.)

• **reassure** them you are there and hold them. Ask for more details about what is going through their minds: "What do you mean?"; "How can I help?"; "I'm so sorry this has happened."

• **let them know** that you will be there for them – reassure them and make sure they know you're not ever going to leave them alone.

• **don't give up** – show them that you're going to be there for them no matter what happens. You can do this by making sure they know that you understand and care.

• **don't promise to do anything that isn't possible** - for example, "I'll never leave you", or "I'll always be here." These are promises that can't be kept, so you will be setting yourself up to fail. If they say that they would rather die than live like this any longer, acknowledge their feelings and tell them it's OK if it really is too much for them to cope with.

• **help them with any practical arrangements** - if they need to go somewhere, let them know when they will be back.

• **call in extra support** – use your support networks to do this. If someone close is over-tired or under-prepared, then ask them if they can help out or take over for a while. This might not be possible but try it anyway. Make sure the person knows that you will be with them throughout the process.

• **offer and show support** – make sure that you know how their family and friends are coping and have ways of talking about the situation calmly if at all possible. Talk to others in the case: "It's not just me going through this. There are other people who also need support".

• **do not be afraid to ask for help** – you won't be the only person going through this. You might feel like you have very little in common with someone going through exactly what you're going through, but it is essential to try and find an insight or commonality between the two of you. This could be as simple as knowing that one of you is a teacher.

• **offer help if anyone approaches you** – don't be afraid to offer your time, skills, and support to whatever individuals need assistance. Let those that want help know that there is always a place for them if they need it.

• **when someone has tried to commit suicide**, make sure that you talk to family or friends about what exactly happened and ensure that they know how they can help. You may need to find a professional counsellor or counsellor to give you the support you need.

As part of your ongoing support, check in with them after a short while. If your loved one has suicidal feelings as part of a break-up between two people, then it's essential that he or she knows that there are lots of people who care about them and who want to help them in whatever way they can.

It's not uncommon for suicidal thoughts to follow a significant life change – so it might be a good idea to check in with them after a short period. Give them some time and space to work out their current situation. And if you think they are at risk, then take action straight away.

It could be that your loved one is feeling low and hurting badly because they think that they have lost the person whom they want to be with. So, you might find it helpful to look at how you can deal with any break-up or loss in the future by reading the relevant sections of this book.

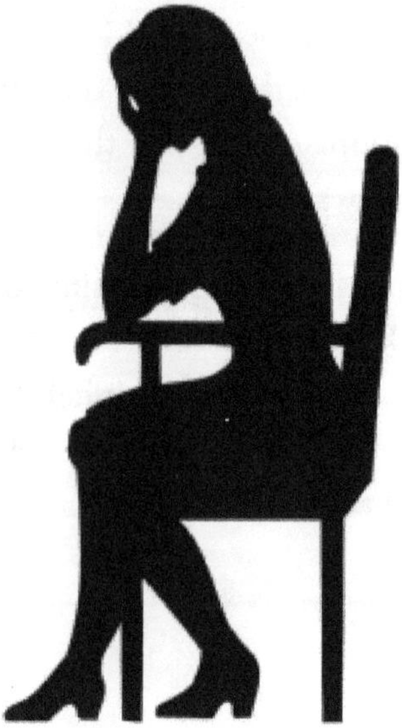

Why Do People Die By Suicide?

Suicide is the deliberate taking of one's life. It can be very devastating, but you must remember that even though your loved one may have taken their own life, they also took the pain from life before that.

Do many people die by suicide?

Yes, many people do die by suicide. And it only appears that your loved one was alone because everyone else around them has to carry on too. Only you understand their last thoughts and how they felt in the final moments of their life.

How long does it take for a person to die by suicide?

The average time to die by suicide is 6 hours. This includes preparing for death and going through the process of dying. You can't tell when it's over, but you can be prepared if you know what to do.

For instance, if your loved one is having problems with pills or alcohol misuse, and they're approaching suicide, try to keep them from using any of these substances.

If your loved one believes they are over-medicated or don't need these prescriptions anymore and have thought about ending their life (in the future), then talk to them about changes in their life that may help reverse the downward spiral.

If you have any of these signs, your loved one may end up dying by suicide.

Why don't people who know about suicide try to save them?

Most people don't want to be the ones to tell someone they mean more than anything else in the world that they have lost their life. They are afraid of losing a loved one's respect as well.

Everyone has their own beliefs, and nothing is meant more than their own life. As a person who knows about suicide, you cannot let anything or anyone take your loved one's place in life. The thoughts of suicide make one feel like they have no other option. They want to be at peace, and they just can't see it happening in life.

What if my loved one loses their life to suicide?

If your loved one loses their life to suicide, you must understand that even though it's a dark place for you right now, you can still live. Life will go on, but your loved one will always be there as well.

Since most of us don't know what it's like to lose a person close to them by suicide, we don't know how it hurts each person differently. You may want revenge because you couldn't do anything about it. Or, you may want to take your own life because you just can't live without them.

The end of your loved one's life is the beginning for others. Your loved one has left their pain behind, and now they are in a place where they are happy and at peace. If your loved one feels this way, they will always be with us in spirit even though they can't walk beside us in everyday life anymore.

Helping Those Who Are Suicidal

Losing a loved one by suicide is a painful experience for most people, but it is not the unfortunate event that it seems to be. Life has many twists and turns, and there are many things that we can do to help a person who has lost his or her loved ones because of suicide.

The Role of Grief in Suicide

Studies have indicated that the decedents were not always at peace with themselves and their life outcomes. According to a study published in the Journal of Affective Disorders, many non-married decedents had severe relationship issues before their suicide. Additionally, a study by Zisook et al. (1998) indicated that before their suicide attempt, the decedents experienced grief and loss that contributed to their depressive states.

The Grief Process after Losing a Loved One by Suicide

As stated previously, people who lose loved ones because they take their own lives go through different emotions during the grieving process. The person can trigger intense feelings in other people. For example, people who are a little bit trigger-happy may shoot themselves, and this may cause an emotional reaction. Similarly, the death of a close friend or family member causes many people to feel overwhelmed.

The way that a person reacts to the grief of losing a loved one is based on his or her approach to grief. Some people may go through the grieving process very quickly, while others take longer. In any case, there are specific steps that everyone goes through during this challenging time:

· **Grief** – Initial denial of death by suicide can lead to denial of guilt; however, this ritualistic behaviour is not healthy and can cause emotional anguish. Waking up each day and not knowing whether a loved one is still alive can lead to an emotional breakdown. Also, this denial can keep a person from grieving for the loss of his or her loved one as he or she would have if he or she acknowledged the death.

· **Anger** – The anger that comes from losing a loved one by suicide has many causes. It is essential to understand why someone took their own life so that you can respond appropriately. For instance, some people may be angry at their loved ones for leaving them without warning, while others are angry at God for taking their loved ones in His hands and not allowing them to suffer any longer.

· **Depression** – Many people who lose their loved ones by suicide lose hope for the future and become more depressed when they visit a funeral home or see someone else who is grieving. This can be prevented by talking to someone about the death of a loved one.

· **Mourning** – There are many rituals that people go through during the grieving process. At first, it is common to sit in silence or walk around and feel anger for not having done anything to prevent the death of a loved one. There is also shock and grief; however, these emotions can be replaced with depression if a person does not deal with them appropriately. The mourning process can be finalized by doing different things that make sense for the person, such as visiting a cemetery with others and talking to them about the deceased.

What should you do if you are around someone who is depressed?

Call a suicide prevention hotline and let them know that you are there for them. If it is a cultural issue, try to understand what they are feeling to support their culture in a way that makes sense to you. If they want attention, give them attention, but they will not get what they want from it. Letting people know that you care about them is essential in this situation because it helps relieve stress and other negative emotions as well as offers emotional support.

The Role of Grief in Suicide

According to studies, a relationship was the most common underlying cause of suicide. Most people who commit suicide do it because of personal problems, such as marital problems or issues with their jobs. In addition to these reasons, others had problems with the law or financial issues that affected them; however, these problems did not directly contribute to their death.

This is why it is crucial to understand why someone took his or her life. If you become aware that something can be corrected, and if they are willing to get treatment for whatever they are experiencing, you may prevent future attempts from being successful.

The Grief Process after Losing a Loved One by Suicide

Talking about death is something that can help many people overcome the grieving process. In addition, this may make them realize that they are not alone and that others are also experiencing the same thing. Additionally, it is essential to understand their relationship with God and share their feelings with Him.

Using Rituals During the Grief Process After Losing a Loved One by Suicide

It is essential to look at rituals as a way of making connections with someone who has died. Rituals can range from prayer to visiting a cemetery or crematory; however, these rituals help people express their grief in a way that makes sense for them. This is a connection with the person that helps them feel closer to him or her.

What Can be Done if You are in the Grief Process After Losing Someone by Suicide?

It is essential to understand that everyone experiences grief differently and that there are things they can do to help themselves through this difficult time:

· **Surround yourself with positive people who make you laugh** – They will ease the pain of losing a loved one and allow you to feel better. You do not have to be around negative or miserable people; however, you must surround yourself with people who make your heart happy.

· **Keep a journal** – Writing down everything you are feeling is not only helpful when you are in the middle of the grief process; it is also vital when you have finished grieving and are ready to move forward.

· **Talk to God** – This one is obvious, but it is essential to remember that talking with God helps ease the pain of losing someone. Some people feel embarrassed or do not know how to speak with an actual person; however, talking to God allows them to get their feelings off their chest and accept them. The problem comes in knowing how to listen because it can be difficult for people who think about themselves most of the time.

· **Join a support group** – This allows people to share their feelings with others who may be experiencing the same thing. It is also important to meet others who have lost a loved one during the same period.

· **Accept the loss** – If you are experiencing the loss of someone who committed suicide, it is essential to remember that you do not have control over what they did, and there is nothing you can do to change their decision. The most important thing at this point is accepting it and moving forward because anything else will only make matters worse for yourself.

· **Take care of your physical health** – Do not forget about your physical health when you are in the middle of grieving. You are likely to lose weight, become malnourished and not eat properly; therefore, it is essential to make sure you are eating and taking care of your body.

The most important thing when it comes to recovering from a loss by suicide is taking your time because there is nothing wrong with grieving over a loved one for however long it takes. It is also important not to forget about the person since this will only make things worse in the long run. This type of loss does not disappear instantly; it takes time, and that is OK. However, you should continue doing healthy activities for yourself, such as taking walks or going on bike rides. Just make sure you are taking care of your body and doing something that makes you feel at peace, so you do not bounce back to business as usual.

If you or a loved one is experiencing loss by suicide, it is essential to know that help is available for those who want it. You can call the 24-hour hotline toll free (find out online) to speak with someone about loss by suicide and all of the ways they can help. You can also visit www.suicidepreventionlifeline.org to find out more about resources in your area that will be able to help if needed.

Can I Ever Get Over The Death Of A Loved One Who Died By Suicide?

I am a bereaved parent who ~~has lost~~ my son. I need some advice on coping with the grief of losing a loved one by suicide, as this is an entirely different experience from other forms of distress.

Dealing With The Grief Of A Suicide Loss My Son Died By Suicide. How Do I Deal With It?

The death of a loved one is always painful, and suicide marks it as unique from all others. The loss becomes not only corporeal but also spiritual and psychological. It can be tough to grieve the death of someone who has taken their own life. There are many reasons why a person may do this, but they have a right to grieve and mourn whatever the reason for their action.

The following article will give you some helpful advice on dealing with the grief of losing a loved one by suicide. By sharing your experiences with others who have also suffered such a loss, you can help others get through this difficult time as much as possible.

Funerals For Suicides

My mother died a year ago today—April 30th, 2015—a suicide. I still don't know how to talk about it. I've tried, but either people don't respond, or they shuffle their feet and change the subject, and I'm not sure which is worse.

We had her funeral today. It was a small, intimate funeral, which we asked for because my mum wouldn't want the 'big' funeral. She never went to funerals—her whole life revolved around where she was and what she was doing at the time. It's something that my entire family has fallen out with over the past four years. We fought about it, and then we made peace. But not everyone came.

A few days ago, I got a text from someone who had known my mother for over thirty years. I never met her, and she never approved of me, but this was her reply to a message I had sent after my mum died:

"Hi, Anna. So sorry to hear that. I hope you are OK. We will not be attending the funeral."

I didn't expect this woman to care or even send condolences, but I did expect some sort of support from her—my mother was, after all, one of her oldest friends—but it wasn't forthcoming.

I can't decide if I want to be mad at her or whether I should just accept it. Either way, she's lost out on a great chance to make amends with me—which is one thing she would have done, only she can't now.

To be honest, it feels like everyone has lost out on a great chance to make amends with me.

All of my close friends have distanced themselves, and I know why. It's nothing personal against me—it's just that no one wants to listen when someone they aren't in close contact with dies. So, we drift apart and stop talking until it becomes too much for us all at once—and then we start again.

My husband has been wonderful, but it's not his family. It's just not the same. He's told me all about them, and I enjoyed learning about them, but it isn't the same as when he does it to one of his family members. It feels like I've become an outsider in my own life—which is a hard feeling for a daughter to bear.

But that's not what this is about.

Writing A Eulogy For Suicide

What are the words to use or not to use? What do you say when the individual who died by their hand was your child, spouse, parent, or close family friend? Can anyone ever be prepared for these heart-wrenching events? How can anyone ever go through this and come out the other side with their sanity and emotional stability intact? When reading about this subject, I came across the term "grieving a death by suicide". I believe that this is very true. It is an entirely different type of grief.

Grief is a combination of sadness and anger. When someone dies by suicide, you are faced with tremendous sorrow and anger. You will often feel guilt, self-blame, anger towards the person who died, along with many more emotions.

Suicide is a permanent solution to a temporary problem. The problem can be depression, addiction or another mental illness. But the solution is permanent and final. No matter what problems that person had in their life, there was always hope that things would get better. This is not so when someone dies by suicide because there was no hope of recovery for the disease/illness/problem they were facing at the time of their decision to end their own life.

Dealing With Such A Tragedy

You must also understand that this process can take many different forms. The individual could have felt that they were not being heard when they were alive. They may have thought there was not enough help around to help them overcome their disease or illness. Or maybe they believed that their only option was to end their lives. Losing a loved one by suicide is more than just the loss of a person. Instead, it is also the loss of someone who has severely injured an entire family, friends and/or community. It is a deep and painful wound that will not heal without time and support.

The grieving process can take many different forms. You can grieve a suicide in different ways at other times. When you first learn about the loss of someone who died by suicide, you may feel as if your world has been turned upside down. The world that was there before has disappeared, leaving in its place a barren wasteland filled with fear, anger, sadness and confusion. However, as you continue to learn about the individual, in time, these feelings may begin to dissipate, and you begin to feel more comfortable with your new reality. Your understanding of what happened will start to fade like the colours on an old faded photograph or torn photo album. You may find yourself feeling nothing but sadness and grief because the person you loved so dearly is now gone.

You may also find yourself feeling as if the world has stopped spinning. It will seem like time has stopped. It will seem like your life has hit a brick wall and is now moving in slow motion. You will walk through everyday life activities, but you won't feel anything inside, and you won't be able to connect with anyone else around you. You will also feel an overwhelming sense of responsibility because you always want to protect everyone from any more loss or pain. You may find yourself struggling with how to help others cope with their new reality. At times you may feel as if you are on the outside looking in at your life. You will often feel as if there is a glass barrier between you and all others around you.

You may find that when someone dies by suicide, this glass barrier completely disappears, and everyone around them is close to you again. You are flooded with love and support from people around you, but they cannot enter your life because the glass barrings are down. You are experiencing a type of grieving where you are completely alone and disconnected from everyone and everything around you. This is called the loss of familiar surroundings.

The most common form of grief experienced by survivors of suicide is the loss of familiar surroundings. It is the thought that everything has changed, but in reality, nothing has changed. The world seems the same as if nothing has happened. It is complicated to accept that someone you loved so dearly is gone forever and that they will never return to be in your life ever again. There will always be reminders or traces that they were here, and they are now gone forever. It remains in place.

The loss of familiar surroundings is one of the most challenging forms of grief to deal with because the world that existed before cannot be replaced or changed. It is as if nothing has happened, as if everything is normal and your loved one has not died. It is an illusion.

You may feel that you are not on your own anymore, and you can now make sense out of things around you. You may feel as if you have found your purpose in life again as if there is a new meaning and purpose to everything around you. You may find that you want to help others recover from this loss because you know how it feels inside so well. You may want to go out and try and connect with others who have lost someone they loved by suicide because you have found a new passion in life.

It is always harder to accept that the person who has died using suicide was suffering from an illness or disease that was not under their control. So, there is no hope for the future, for the possibility of recovery or improvement. This can be as cruel as losing a loved one using death by another disease. It cuts down on any hope or potential for change in the future.

You may find that you become very angry with the illness or disease that took your loved one's life for destroying a part of your life and out of your control. You will also remain angry with yourself for a long time because you feel like you have failed to be a good friend or loved one. This is because you cannot understand how someone who was once entirely in your life could wreck it overnight by taking their own life.

The most common feeling experienced by survivors of suicide is loss of control and confusion. It can feel like your soul has been ripped out through your stomach, leaving you empty inside. It can feel as if your mind has been grasped tightly, and your thoughts cannot easily come out. You have lost your clarity of thought. It is difficult to make decisions and think through things logically.

You may mourn the loss of a significant part of yourself that you can never get back again or just the loss of the best friend you ever had in life. You may also mourn the fact that someone so close to you could leave so quickly without any warning or explanation. The thought that they were suffering from a disease or illness for such a long time kept them from being able to let someone know they were slowly slipping away into death's arms one day at a time.

Stages Of Grief By Suicide

What are the stages of grief for a suicidal death?

The stages of grief after a death by suicide are similar for people who have lost a friend or family member to the act.

The stages of grief are as follows:

- *Denial*
- *Anger*
- *Bargaining*
- *Depression and remorse.*

After a death, it is normal to experience anger. With this comes the need to ask why such things happen and how they could have been stopped. This leads to the question of should more be done to prevent such events from happening, and if so, what can be done?

In one case, a married couple had a history of domestic violence. The wife was angry at her husband for abusing her. One evening she took an overdose of pills and died in the home in front of their four-year-old child. There was no note or other evidence that this event was related to the abuse that she suffered. The family had no history or history of death from suicide in their family line by any means prior to this incident.

Bargaining

Bargaining is the stage where people try to negotiate with God, the deceased or both. They will promise anything in exchange for not having to go through the pain of the grief. This stage includes thoughts such as "I'll never drink again if you let my loved one come back". This stage may last a long time and involves many souls searching.

In one case, a young man was a student at an Ivy League school when he committed suicide after a career-ending injury. He left behind a girlfriend and loving family and friends who were devastated by his death. His parents wanted to know why he did it and why they couldn't have seen it coming. They had to live with the thought that they could have prevented this.

Depression

Depression is characterized by long periods of crying, inability to sleep and feelings of despair. In some cases, anger and sadness may alternate for weeks or months prior to acceptance.

In one case, a woman who was diagnosed with cancer died by suicide. She ended her life when her health started to deteriorate rapidly, and she became dependent on others rather than being able to care for herself and other family members. At the time of death, her mother was taking care of her in the home where she lived with two daughters under ten years old. The mother and daughter were stunned by the suicide and were not prepared to deal with it.

Acceptance

Acceptance is when one can finally accept the reality of the event. This stage is more than simply accepting that a life has ended. Acceptance means that one has either accepted death or accepts a new way of life where the thoughts of suicide are not present.

In one case, a boy who was three years old committed suicide by hanging himself in his own closet. His father was convinced it was an accident until he began to suspect foul play when he noticed "*traps*" had been set along the child's path home. He discovered the location of the child's body when investigating what was happening in the household. After he refused to become involved in his son's life, the mother became despondent and moved out, leaving her with no other support than a grandmother.

What can parents do?

The first question to answer is "*why*?"

When someone commits suicide, remember that they are thinking through their own feelings and experiences. In many cases, family members may not find out what happened until months later when automatic bank withdrawals from checking accounts begin or a loved one is found dead in an unexpected situation. Many people are not as upset by a death by suicide as they are by deaths at the home of accidents or natural causes that could have been prevented.

Exploring the reasons why an individual feels a need to end it all can help people understand their loved ones better and prevent similar acts in the future.

The most important thing that parents can do is to have an open dialogue with their teen and be sure they understand that there is a problem. Parents should be discussing suicidal thoughts such as "*If you are going through this, how am I going make it through*?" or "*What do you want to do when you get out of high school*?" Often these discussions arise from different pressures or troubles that a teen may be experiencing.

A parent should also discuss a plan of action in case of an emergency as well as providing counselling for themselves or friends if they need it.

In one case, a teen boy was hit by a car injuring his leg and making it difficult for him to keep up with friends and chores. He became withdrawn and felt he was "losing his social life." His mother did not understand why he was behaving in this way, thinking that he should just get over it. His father wrestled with feelings of hurt that his son would rather be with friends than spend time with him. When the boy tried to run away from home, his father discovered a note in the boy's pocket stating that he planned to run away and never come back. At this point, the father called 911 as well as the boy's counsellor. The boy was brought to the hospital, where his injuries were seen to be serious. The boy had tried to take an overdose of pills and would have died if he had not been taken to the hospital in time.

If a parent, teacher or coach suspects suicide, they should contact a suicide hotline or call emergency police and let the emergency response team know that they are concerned about someone's wellbeing.

Counselling is available today to help families and friends cope with the loss.

There are resources that have been set up to help parents deal with their emotions and anxieties when dealing with suicide. It is vital for parents and family members to search for supportive services in order to overcome the trauma that can accompany a death by suicide.

To conclude, there is no easy way when coping with the loss of a loved one by suicide. Everyone is different and deals with their feelings in a variety of ways. Find what suits you best, and take your time to grieve. The loss will take time but it does get better over time as you have read earlier from some of the comments of those who have lost their loved ones too.

Ask God to help you through your trials, he will strengthen you if you ask him. The next section provides you with some helpful bible scriptures concerning grief and loss. Meditate upon them when you feel burdened and overwhelmed, especially when you have quiet moments.

God Can Help With Your Loss

Here are some helpful bible scriptures to help and comfort you in your loss:

"The Lord is close to the brokenhearted; he rescues those whose spirits are crushed."

- Psalm 34:18

"Don't be afraid, for I am with you. Don't be discouraged, for I am your God. I will strengthen you and help you. I will hold you up with my victorious right hand."

– Isaiah 41:10

"God blesses those who mourn, for they will be comforted."

-Matthew 5:4

"God is our refuge and strength, always ready to help in times of trouble."

-Psalm 46:1

"Be still, and know that I am God! I will be honoured by every nation. I will be honoured throughout the world."

- Psalm 46:10

"He will wipe every tear from their eyes, and there will be no more death or sorrow or crying or pain. All these things are gone forever."

- Revelation 21:4

"Give all your worries and cares to God, for he cares about you."

- 1 Peter 5:7

"You keep track of all my sorrows. You have collected all my tears in your bottle. You have recorded each one in your book."

- Psalm 56:8

"You light a lamp for me. The Lord, my God, lights up my darkness."

- Psalm 18:28

"And this same God who takes care of me will supply all your needs from his glorious riches, which have been given to us in Christ Jesus."

- Philippians 4:19

Gospel = Good News!

Good To Be True News

Corinthians 15:1-4

Your loved one has gone straight up to heaven with the Lord.

You will see them again in eternal life up in heaven. None of us is promised our last breath. But the good news is that you, too, can be saved with God's free gift. Time is short; get saved, seek Jesus today!

Here's how:

ABC Of Salvation

A - ADMIT

Admit you are a sinner and have made

mistakes.

Romans 3:23

B - BELIEVE

Believe that Jesus is God's son, died on the Cross for you, and rose up from the grave on the third day.

Romans 10:9-10

C - CONFESS

Confess with your mouth that Jesus is

Lord of your life. Commit yourself to a life of following Jesus and serving others.

Romans 10:13

Thank you for your purchase.

I hope you found the information in this book to be of value, help and comfort.

If so, please give us a thumbs-up; your review is essential to us to assist others in their journey.

I am thanking you in advance.

About The Author

Anthea Peries BSc (Hons) is a published author; she completed her undergraduate studies in several sciences, including Biology, Brain and Behaviour and Child Development.

A graduate member of the British Psychological Society, she has experience in counselling and is a former senior management executive.

Born in London, Anthea enjoys fine cuisine, writing and has travelled the world. She has a spoilt but cute, naughty black and white cat named Giorgio.

Other Books By This Author

You may be interested in other self-help books by Anthea Peries, particularly about bereavement, funerals, grief journals, chemotherapy treatment, other areas such as eating disorders, food addiction, binge-eating, sugar cravings, emotional eating or, night eating syndrome, insomnia.

Don't miss out!

Visit the website below and you can sign up to receive emails whenever Anthea Peries publishes a new book. There's no charge and no obligation.

https://books2read.com/r/B-A-DMCG-DPVOB

Also by Anthea Peries

Cancer and Chemotherapy

Coping with Cancer & Chemotherapy Treatment: What You Need to Know to Get Through Chemo Sessions

Coping with Cancer: How Can You Help Someone with Cancer, Dealing with Cancer Family Member, Facing Cancer Alone, Dealing with Terminal Cancer Diagnosis, Chemotherapy Treatment & Recovery

Chemotherapy Survival Guide: Coping with Cancer & Chemotherapy Treatment Side Effects

Eating Disorders

Food Cravings: Simple Strategies to Help Deal with Craving for Sugar & Junk Food

Sugar Cravings: How to Stop Sugar Addiction & Lose Weight

The Immune System, Autoimmune Diseases & Inflammatory Conditions: Improve Immunity, Eating Disorders & Eating for Health

Food Addiction: Overcome Sugar Bingeing, Overeating on Junk Food & Night Eating Syndrome

Food Addiction: Overcoming your Addiction to Sugar, Junk Food, and Binge Eating
Food Addiction: Why You Eat to Fall Asleep and How to Overcome Night Eating Syndrome
Overcome Food Addiction: How to Overcome Food Addiction, Binge Eating and Food Cravings
Healthy Gut: Transform Your Health from the Inside Out, for a Healthy You
Emotional Eating: Stop Emotional Eating & Develop Intuitive Eating Habits to Keep Your Weight Down
Emotional Eating: Overcoming Emotional Eating, Food Addiction and Binge Eating for Good
Eating At Night Time: Sleep Disorders, Health and Hunger Pangs: Tips On What You Can Do About It

Food Addiction

Overcoming Food Addiction to Sugar, Junk Food. Stop Binge Eating and Bad Emotional Eating Habits
Food Addiction: Overcoming Emotional Eating, Binge Eating and Night Eating Syndrome
Weight Loss Without Dieting: 21 Easy Ways To Lose Weight Naturally

Grief, Bereavement, Death, Loss

Coping with Loss & Dealing with Grief: Surviving Bereavement, Healing & Recovery After the Death of a Loved One

How to Plan a Funeral
Coping With Grief And Heartache Of Losing A Pet: Loss Of A Beloved Furry Companion: Easing The Pain For Those Affected By Animal Bereavement
Grieving The Loss Of Your Baby: Coping With The Devastation Shock And Heartbreak Of Losing A Child Through Miscarriage, Still Birth

Health Fitness
How To Avoid Colds and Flu Everyday Tips to Prevent or Lessen The Impact of Viruses During Winter Season

Quark Cheese
50 More Ways to Use Quark Low-fat Soft Cheese: The Natural Alternative When Cooking Classic Meals
Quark Cheese Recipes: 21 Delicious Breakfast Smoothie Ideas Using Quark Cheese
30 Healthy Ways to Use Quark Low-fat Soft Cheese

Relationships
The Grief Of Getting Over A Relationship Breakup: How To Accept Breaking Up With Your Ex | Advice And Tips To Move On

Sleep Disorders

Sleep Better at Night and Cure Insomnia Especially When Stressed

Standalone

Family Style Asian Cookbook: Authentic Eurasian Recipes: Traditional Anglo-Burmese & Anglo-Indian

Coping with Loss and Dealing with Grief: The Stages of Grief and 20 Simple Ways on How to Get Through the Bad Days

Coping With Grief Of A Loved One After A Suicide: Grieving The Devastation And Loss Of Someone Who Took Their Own Life. How Long Does The Heartache Last?

About the Author

Anthea Peries BSc (Hons) is a published author, she completed her undergraduate studies in several branches of the sciences including Biology, Neurology, Brain and Behaviour and Child Development. A former graduate member of the British Psychological Society, she has experience in counselling and is a former senior management executive. Born in London, Anthea enjoys fine cuisine, writing, and has travelled the world.

Printed in the USA
CPSIA information can be obtained
at www.ICGtesting.com
LVHW090736010624
781988LV00008B/203

9 798201 205553